Grand Benefit

SUSAN HOFFMAN

Grand Benefit

If grandparent visitation is simply beneficial
then taking it away is quite simply harmful.

SUSAN HOFFMAN

Print ISBN 978-0-9799168-7-8
Collegare Press

Author Photo By Lawrence Sherwin
Book Design by BeAPurplePenguin.com

CONTENTS

CHAPTER 1
Benefit vs Harm ◆ 7

CHAPTER 2
Memories ◆ 9

CHAPTER 3
Broken Connections ◆ 15

CHAPTER 4
Consequences ◆ 29

CHAPTER 5
Advocacy ◆ 33

CHAPTER 6
Wyoming: A Window Into Going To Court ◆ 37

CHAPTER 7
More About State Laws ◆ 47

CHAPTER 8
Why We Need Advocacy ◆ 57

CHAPTER 9
Quality verses Quantity ◆ 63

CHAPTER 10
Boundaries ◆ 69

CHAPTER 11
Reasons to deny ◆ 75

CHAPTER 12
Going To Court ◆ 81

CHAPTER 13
My Case ◆ 85

CHAPTER 14
Parental Authority And Case Precedence ◆ 95

CHAPTER 15
Family Law Attorney Contributes ◆ 105

CHAPTER 16
Grandparent Alienation Syndrome ◆ 107

CHAPTER 17
Words Of Wisdom ◆ 113

CHAPTER 18
Some Things To Think About ◆ 119

CHAPTER 19
Conclusion ◆ 125

OTHER BOOKS BY
Susan Hoffman ◆ 129

ABOUT THE AUTHOR
Susan Hoffman ◆ 131

CHAPTER 1

Benefit vs Harm

HOW CAN TAKING a loving adult away from a child not cause harm? I mean isn't that kind of common sense? But just try and prove it.

There is absolutely harm caused to a child when a grandparent is taken away from them—or any loving adult, for that matter, with whom they have engendered a bond.

The truth is children need all of the love that they can get in order to thrive. A Grand Benefit is it's the grandparent who provides a huge source of that love. Building self-esteem is a vital part of growth. A complete and confident human being evolves through feelings of security beginning with feeling loved. Knowing that you're loved by all the adults in your life creates the foundation of believing that you're okay. Self-esteem is an ongoing process that must be nurtured. It's not a one and done situation, something Dr. Lillian Carson has spoken publicly about as well as written on the subject in her book, *The Essential Grandparent* (Health Communications Inc. 1996).

A grandparent is the perfect adult to assume the job of providing unconditional love toward a grandchild.

A grandparent is the perfect adult to assume the job of providing nurturing that comes from desire and not obligation.

A grandparent is the perfect person to assume the job of providing stability.

A grandparent is the perfect adult to assume the job of providing familial history. After all, isn't that their role?

Grandparents being the parents of the parents and next of kin to the child are the most likely people to possess a natural bond. The mutual love between a grandparent and grandchild is like no other and the bond should never be severed. Ever. And when unfortunate circumstances arise creating a threat to that bond beyond the control of the grandparent and grandchild it will always cause harm. It will cause harm to the child and to the grandparent.

As a side note, there will always be situations where children require distance from certifiably dangerous adults for their own protection. This is book is not about that issue.

CHAPTER 2

Memories

IT DIDN'T MATTER that he was my grandpa by marriage and not blood. What did matter is that he was my rock. I called him by his first name, Coy. As the only kid living in a household of three adults, I was treated as one. I was Included in everything and with little attention to conversational censorship by adults, I picked up on how the land lies pretty quickly.

We never missed "Gunsmoke" and "Roller Derby" on Saturday nights. Our TV night menu consisted of shiny big red apples followed by a bowl of chocolate chip ice cream.

My fondest childhood memories are of the time spent with my grandparents. My mother and I lived with her mom, Blanche and stepdad, Coy for five years before they ended up moving to a neighboring city so they could be closer to work. I was in nursery school by then and spent every weekend with them since I no longer saw them on a daily basis.

Every summer they took me along on their vacations. We piled into the big white Chevy station wagon and set off on road trips to just about every state with the exception of the east coast and Canadian border states.

With the windows always rolled down—probably no air-conditioning—Blanche would rest her arm on the lowered window atop the door and by the end of the trip that arm was so dark from the sun she had a mismatched set of white and brown arms. I can't say that I recall her evening it up by taking a turn at driving, though.

We drove from Los Angeles to Texas to visit Coy's mother and father one summer. Everyone there talked different, which was fascinating to me. It was the first time I had heard a southern accent. Although Blanche had remnants of an Oklahoma dialect now and then, occasionally dropping her "g's" and syllables running words together.

Coy's folks had a few small animals, like a real live bunny that I got to play with. I loved it so much the parents said that I could have it only it had to stay put.

Our local trips mostly consisted of visiting outdoor places in California like Sequoia, National Park, which was a favorite with all of those big redwood trees that you could drive through. We sometimes stayed in rustic cabins in the mountains where we would have to walk to the park restrooms, and once we even came across a bear. I didn't see it because it was dark, but Blanche claimed she felt it brush up against her leg and then she yanked me by the arm forcing us to start running fast to the cabin.

I remember when we rented a house on the sand in Long Beach and that time my mom came too. We all loved the beach and went almost every weekend for day trips to local places like El Porto and El Segundo. I remember standing between my grandparents in the front seat in anticipation of glimpsing that first vision of the Pacific Ocean. Each time the street began to descend toward the beach it was like the first time, giving me a thrill of excitement to see that giant blue body of water.

There was another set of grandparents too. Lucky me. Even though my mom and dad divorced when I was a baby I got to keep his family. The best part of my parents' marriage was my grandparents.

Since everybody worked in my household, my paternal grandma took care of me for a while before I started nursery school and since she didn't drive we rode the bus or streetcars in Los Angeles. As the child of divorced parents, I usually got two of everything. My grandparents put on their own birthday parties for me when I was small so that they could be more of a part of my life. They were always so happy to see me.

It's because of their efforts that I somehow knew at a young age that they were always there even though I didn't get to see them as much once my mom remarried.

I still miss all of my grandparents and sometimes I dream about them. Sadly, Coy died young in his late 40's and Blanche was in her 70's. But my paternal grandfather lived into his 80's and my grandma was 102 when she died.

I began to spend more time with my paternal grandparents as an adult. One of my first jobs was at Bullocks Department store in La Habra, California. The Fashion Square mall was nearby to my grandparents' house and I would run over on my dinner break when I worked nights and enjoy a home cooked meal with them. They usually ate at 4:30 in the afternoon, but would alter their schedule to accommodate my work time. I appreciated them more and wanted to make up for the time lost during my childhood after my mother remarried.

Later on, when I had my own children, it was my own grandparents that I wanted them to be close to. They were the most stable role models in my life. My mom and her husband were not stable, which often is the problem when a non-biological person is brought into a family. It changes the dynamics. And my in-laws lived further away and didn't seem as interested in forming a close bond since it was a big family and they had so many other grandchildren.

Whenever we had to leave our child, it was my grandparents that we called upon. I trusted them more than anyone with my child. We even took them on trips, sometimes to help with babysitting, other times just to spend time with them. All those years while I was eating up the attention bestowed upon me, it was actually unconditional love that I was given.

"Grandparents are the best kind of grownups."

— Unknown

CHAPTER 3

Broken Connections

MY CLOSE BOND with my grandparents was a natural part of growing up; not an uncommon theme with families. The vital importance of sustaining that connection is why I created a charitable organization that advocates on behalf of the grandparent-grandchild relationship. The grandparents who seek our support are sadly those who have suffered lost access or a threat of losing access to a grandchild. Since this happened to me when I became a grandparent it propelled me into activism.

Children are not chattel and shouldn't be used as a bargaining chip or pawn. Sometimes adults don't see eye to eye, which has nothing to do with kids. Yet they are the ones who are punished the most by adult discord.

CARMEN

A grandmother from Connecticut had great difficulty spending time with her three year old grandson following the death of her daughter, the child's mother. The parents had been divorced and the father assumed full custody upon his former wife's death.

The visits with the grandson over the next four years were tightly controlled by the dad. He had always harbored resentment about the divorce and now took it out on the grandmother. He kept her away for a year and finally relented to supervised coffee shop visits for Christmas gifts or a pizza parlor for birthday gifts. The child always made sure that his grandmother be seated next to him, saying, "sit here," as soon as he saw her.

It took a snowstorm to alter the routine. When Grandma offered shelter for her grandson and his father during a power outage it softened the father's resolve. When the dad and grandmother took Sawyer shopping for snow boots the next day, he pulled his grandmother aside and whispered, "let's hide."

When it was time to go back home, Sawyer began sobbing refusing to let go of his grandmother. His father interceded, saying, "If you cry then Honey (grandmother's given nickname by the child) can't come here again." A perfect example of stifling emotions.

When Sawyer was fourteen, following a visit with his grandmother before she returned to her second home in South Carolina, he begged her, "Honey don't leave." He later told his father, everything he loves, he loses. He ended up in the hospital after cutting himself more than once. Grandmother Honey moved back to Connecticut permanently after that. Sawyer received therapy and ultimately graduated from high school. The tightly controlled environment by the father, even at seventeen years old, created frustration over lack of freedom. Sawyer expressed his feelings to his grandmother, saying, "I just can't wait to get out of this place, he's so demanding, I'm fed up." As Sawyer's grandmother, Honey provided a source of support and comfort; a sounding board, a safe place to vent and be heard. Plus she was the only direct link to his mother.

"Since my return, Sawyer has improved dramatically. He hasn't done any self-harm, and has evened out completely," said Honey. "We purchased a car for him and he was accepted to college in Massachusetts. He spends many weekends at my home where he has a room and private sitting area. "I am a sounding board to him. I am a grandmother who although I don't approve of the things he's done, I support him while still offering my unsolicited advice. My love for him is unconditional."

Sawyer, now 19, still shares his feelings with his grandmother, "having phone conversations helps us both, regardless of his age."

"I share this with you to show the downward spiral that Sawyer was subjected to by his forced isolation from his grandparents. I believe the isolation led to self-harm and institutionalization and which was only rectified upon my full-time reinsertion into his life at that critical time."

While Carmen (A.K.A. Honey) feels fortunate now to have her devoted grandson Sawyer, back in her life, it wasn't without a fight. Around 2008, not long after the alienation, Carmen joined the Connecticut task force to lobby for better grandparent laws. It didn't move the cause. She'd also filed a petition for visitation out of fear that the loss would lead to mental health issues; that Sawyer would think his grandparents did not love him and was not worthy of their affection. The parental-like role and harm factor stood in the way in the eyes of the law.

Excerpt from Carmen's 2009 testimonial on behalf of the Connecticut Human Services Committee to establish a task force on Grandparents rights for visitation:

> "In March of 2007, when my daughter relapsed of leukemia, my husband and I immediately relocated to her home in Connecticut where we not only cared for her, but also for her three and a half year old son—my grandson.
>
> "On November 21, 2007, the day my 34 year old daughter passed away, my grandson suffered a blow of damaging proportion. My daughter previously had a bone marrow transplant even though her chances of

survival were 5 to 10%, she decided to take her chances with the treatment. She often told us and her doctors that she did this only for her son. She feared leaving him behind.

My husband and I had had a beautiful loving relationship with our grandson. We were at the hospital to welcome him into the world. We would come to Connecticut and stay with both my daughter and my grandson four months out of the year. During that period, we would take our grandson for walks, sledding, haircuts, donuts, swimming and go on vacations together—all the traditional things that loving grandparents do.

It would put a smile on my daughter's face to see the emotional attachment that her son shared with us. She would comment about the strong bond we cherished with her son. She wanted us to have life-long ties with her son; same as she had with her grandparents. She would take her son to visit his great-grandmother every Sunday—they would have supper there.

Research shows that losing a parent is the number one cause of stress for children. Losing a grandparent is the number five cause of stress for children. After three years in my grandson's life, upon losing his mother, my grandson lost his "Pa" (grandpa) and to a great extent his "Honey" (me).

Shortly after my daughter's passing, I told the dad, I wanted to preserve the relationship I had with my grandson: that I was willing to take care of him either after, before or instead of daycare. The dad told me that my grandson "does not need to be mothered."

I have been repeatedly told by my grandson's father that he DOES NOT have to commit to visits between me and my four year old grandson.

In 2008 we purchased my daughter's condo in Connecticut in hopes of continuing our loving relationship with our grandson. That year I was able to see my grandson for a total of 16 1/2 hours, always closely supervised by his dad at his home.

My grandson cries when I am ready to leave and it breaks my heart because I cannot tell him when I will be able to see him again. I sense a great deal of emotional stress on his part. He will ask me to please stay a little bit longer. He will take off my shoes. He tells me that I am not going to see him for a long time; he has told me that his dad has told him that he will never be able to go to his mom's house. I am paralyzed after hearing his words. I feel that visits with my grandson would help reduce any emotional harm or suffering that he may experience.

My grandson's formative years are at stake. I want to be a part of my grandson's childhood. To walk away from his life, **which is what his dad wants and the CT state law expects me to do,** would be to diminish the meaning of my daughter's life. I have a moral obligation to them.

The time being wasted by taking my case to court puts me at a disadvantage with the dad. It has made the dad more determined to deny me access-because the law allows it. Meanwhile my grandson suffers the loss of the love, care and support of his maternal grandparents. I am not interested in custody or control over my grandson's life. I just want to reasonably visit with him.

Connecticut needs a viable solution that would work in the best interest of the child. The law in CT is assuming that the surviving parent(s) is acting in the child's best interest. But in my grandson's case, his voice and his concerns are not being heard by his dad. He has no rights and neither do

> I, his grandmother. My daughter's death should not grant the father the right to sever a positive and loving relationship.
>
> My grandson should have the right to have his maternal grandparents in his life—it is what his mother, my daughter wanted and what my grandson deserves. Nature took his mom away from him but the state of Connecticut should not prevent his maternal grandparent from reasonable visitation with him.
>
> Next time you visit with your grandchild, if just for one moment, can you think of my four year old grandson, who lost his mom, his "Pa" and to a great extent his grandmother, me.
>
> You can help. Please act to begin the process to give grandparents reasonable access to their grandchildren. Only my grandson knows what it feels like not to have all these people that love him in his life."

DEB

In another example, it was the daughter-in-law who stepped in to put the brakes on Grandma Deb (A.K.A. Nunnie) having visits with her three year old grandson, Brady. Her son went along with the decision in order to keep the peace.

Grandma Deb, waited it out for a couple of months, hoping the parents would come around. When they didn't she took matters into her own hands. She was worried sick that Brady would wonder why she suddenly disappeared.

Being familiar with the family routine, she knew that Brady would be up early by himself while watching cartoons in the living room, which also had a large window facing the street. At six a.m. on a Saturday morning she pulled up to the house hoping that Brady would see her. He did. He flung open the door and ran toward her car, shouting "Nunnie, Nunnie, I miss you," as he climbed inside. "Why don't you come and play with me anymore?" "I won't be bad, I'll be good. Please come and play with me."

Most of their car visit was spent with Deb doing damage control about her absence and promising to return the following Saturday. The second Saturday, Brady's dad caught them. The dad ultimately allowed them to finish reading the book after seeing how content the child was, how much he was enjoying the car visit with his grandmother.

As it turned out the car visits continued for sixteen months, each ending with Brady crying and not wanting to leave his Nunnie.

The reconciliation between mother and son occurred when he showed up on her doorstep with Brady in tow and announced that his marriage was over. Upon seeing the interaction of his dad and grandmother Brady threw his flip flop at his dad and shouted," don't you ever take me away from my Nunnie again!"

CAROL AND GREG

In the third example, nearly three months had passed since Grammy Carol and Papa Greg had seen their six year old granddaughter Michaela, as a result of the mother's anger directed at the grandparents.

What followed was a petition for court ordered visitation on behalf of the grandparents. The court case drug on for months until a temporary order was granted by the judge for monitored monthly visits. The child had a hard time understanding the unnatural environment and strict timeline. She begged to go to the grandparents' house instead. She sobbed when the visits were over as the allotted time came to an end. The court ordered visits alternated between a time span of four hours and ten. This was frustrating for a child who couldn't understand the restrictions and why they couldn't go back to Grammy and Papa's house.

Children are sometimes told things by their parents that aren't true when they are asked where the grandparents are. Michaela confided in her grammy that she thought that they forgot about her after her mother revealed that the grandparents didn't have time for her anymore.

"Because we won the case, the connection wasn't

broken and the bond continued to grow," said Grammy Carol. "She is now nineteen and the older she gets, she still includes us."

LANA

Lana's son and daughter-in-law found an opportunity to become offended at the grandparents and even though they lived less than a mile away, they decided to take an extended break from the grandparents. The reasons were petty compared to the emotional consequences. The child was three years old when this occurred. The grandparents were devastated and didn't know where to turn.

One day I received a call from the grandfather's secretary asking about my book, Grand Wishes. Not wanting to wait for it to be shipped, the grandfather ended up meeting me in the parking lot of my spin class that evening. He said they had been looking for support and information about grandparent rights and had found our organization after searching the Internet. They were grateful to have found us and to learn that we also offered in person support group meetings at OASIS Senior Center in Corona del Mar not far from where they lived.

The grandmother attended every monthly meeting. She was always open to suggestion about adopting new ways to build specific communication skills that would benefit her situation and help her reconnect with the parents.

She received support, education, information and hands on coaching. We helped her carefully draft and compose letters to the parents to let them know the grandparents weren't going away. Staying in touch also paved the way toward a more welcoming environment should the parents respond. It's kind of a way of saving face. Keeping the fires burning sends the message that all is forgiven.

Then the door began to open after Lana's granddaughter, Presley had been at a kindergarten classmate's birthday party where grandparents were present. Her dad, who had also been there, overheard Presley say in an envious tone, "Oh you have a grandma," to the child who was having the party.

That had been a wake up call for the dad, who began to realize the disservice the denial of grandparents had put upon their daughter. Shortly after, the parents and grandparents reconciled. After the three year absence they met at a park. The first the thing Presley did was grab the grandma's hand and say, " Come on, let's play."

The son apologized.

Presley now 16 years old lives with her grandparents along with her dad who has been separated from the mom. Presley has relayed some of the terrible things that were said in the past by her mother about the grandparents. She has since vowed never to go back to her mother's home again.

SUSAN

My personal experience was a roller coaster. I was in and then I was out since Jacob had been five years old, something I have written about since 2008.

It was a tug of war the way Jacob was thrust in the middle of his parent's contentious divorce causing him to be out of my life again until his mid-teens. After three years of separation, the first time until age eight, when his adoptive dad let me back into his life until the gavel came down again on our renewed relationship of eight months. Then six years later we reconnected when he was a teenager and have been together ever since. We had to start over.

Our relationship was forever changed after so many gaps. How could it not be? There was so much lost time we'll never get back. He is a fine young man, kind, caring and focused on his future endeavors. He has relocated in another state and no longer lives near his family. We are a work in progress and continue moving forward to fill the void and repair the damage created by a fractured relationship. I've lived the damage. Time is the most important thing we have and when you take away time, you take away everything. The result is HARM.

"Grandmas hold our tiny hands for just a little while…but our hearts forever."

—Unknown

CHAPTER 4

Consequences

WHILE THERE ARE no statistics, or published research about the amount of harm caused to a child when they have been purposefully denied access to a grandparent, there is a recent study that sheds some light on the subject. In Bereavement & mental health: The generational consequences of a grandparent's death, (Michelle Livings, Emily Smith Greenaway, Aston Verdery, and Rachel Margolis (SSM-Mental Health, Science Direct, December 2022.) The study consisted of the long-lasting mental health effects resulting from the loss of a grandparent to death. The research shows that grandparents' involvement in a grandchild's life plays a critically important role in a child's overall health and development. The 2022 study stated that the death of a grandmother can have not only severe, but lasting mental health consequences for both adult children and grandchildren.

The researchers observed the results could be seen as somewhat surprising since the death of a grandparent is an anticipated and normal part of life. They wrote, "Yet the results are profound. Losing a grandparent can increase adolescents' risk of having a depressed parent and of having higher depressive symptoms themselves."

The study went on to cite the fact that grandparents' involvement and support has been shown in decades of research to be ***beneficial*** to their grandchildren. Also many grandparents act as a safety net for the grandkids, benefiting a grandchild's health and development when they are living in a home with a single mother.

While the study covered other factors, the relevancy is that adolescent mental health has worsened in recent decades. Depression rates will increase in the U.S. because of the dramatic number of grieving adolescents.

Gathering information about emotional consequences of broken relationships between grandparents and grandchildren requires discovery. Being there is the only way to discover what is truly going on with the child's present emotional well-being. Grandparents who have established consistent visits with grandkids have an advantage of better understanding when changes occur. For example when visits come to an end it isn't such a traumatic experience saying good-bye when they feel the security of knowing the grandparents will be back. But when there is a sudden change and the period of separation between the child and the grandparents becomes obscure that can bring about sadness and insecurity for the child when it's time to part. There's that unknown bewilderment that a child senses of not knowing when they will see the grandparents again. A similar situation is the tension that frequently accompanies a court-ordered visitation schedule. Saying good-bye to grandparents becomes a stressful emotional and sad experience because that security of knowing they will see them soon is gone. Kids pick up on familial discord, which influences their emotional status. When this occurs, and grandparents are at the mercy of limited amounts of time, it's hard to learn what's going on with the child.

The longest period of waiting to learn about the child's feelings brought on by grandparent separation is when they finally re-connect, sometimes when the child reaches the age of 18 years. Even then, you may not ever know their feelings. You will after some time, though, observe their behavior and get to understand how they are.

During a child custody or visitation court case a forensic psychologist is retained to provide an evaluation. But then again the outcome is based on limited sessions with a stranger. A grandparent who has spent quality time with a grandchild is more likely to evaluate what's going on over time. A grandchild who has lived through the experience is the most accurate witness to their own feelings.

"There's no place like home—
except grandma's house."

—Unknown

CHAPTER 5

Advocacy

ADVOCATING MEANS ACTIVELY addressing and supporting the importance of sustaining that precious bond that exists between grandparent and grandchild. Advocating means actively addressing and supporting access in the first place so that the opportunity is present to cultivate a relationship into such a bond. Shouldn't grandparents at least be given a chance to meet their grandchild? Shouldn't a child at least be given a chance to know their grandparent?

Taking away someone that you love and have established a bond with should never happen. But never having the opportunity in the first place at giving and receiving that love is...well, reprehensible.

Parents and custodial caregivers are serving their child's emotional well-being by providing access to loving adults. There can never be too many adults in a child's life who love them.

All 50 states and D.C. currently have some type of "grandparent visitation rights" statutes. Grandparent visitation rights statutes do not automatically guarantee that they will have any type of parental responsibility or have legal rights to see grandchildren unless there's a court order in place. Even then there's the issue of enforceability of the order. Parents have authority to decide who the child may see. Parents have authority to raise a child as they see fit. PARENTAL AUTHORITY. Period.

Some states have restrictive laws meaning the conditions have a narrow perimeter and are specific. For example, familial status (divorce, death, nuclear or non-intact family situations), the existence of a substantial relationship between the child and grandparent, the fitness of the parent as well as that of the petitioning grandparent, the requirement for grandparents to rebut the presumption of a finding for the parents, adoptions and so on.

Others being less restrictive may include a broad field such as the best interests criteria. And some states include provisions with extreme conditions like emphasizing time as a qualification measurement. In other words grandparents were supposed to have served in a parent-like role of the grandchild. The "harm" factor is another extreme condition, which places a heavy burden on the grandparents to provide proof of the ways that the child will endure harm when visitation is denied with the grandparent. And how does one prove fitness of a parent? Another obstacle to overcome. I mean why so many hoops to jump through just to love a child?

Again, in my opinion it's common sense that removing a loving grandparent with whom the child has established a bond is extremely harmful to the child's emotional state. But that common sense gets thrown out the window once it becomes an issue in the court of law.

The simple act of loving a child and the child loving a grandparent should not be that hard. What exactly is the harm caused to the child in letting the grandparent continue to be a part of their lives? Children are central and their needs should be considered above all else, it doesn't matter what's going on with adults. With parental authority in place the parents can certainly monitor the relationship. The parents can establish visitation boundaries without creating World War III.

Allowing the natural flow is a positive step. Disrupting becomes a take away, a negative step. Again, what's the Harm in allowing visits? Do what it takes, make adjustments to make it happen. Why stir the pot to begin with, why remove and create Harm? Instead, don't do Harm to begin with.

"You are the sun, Grandma, you are the sun in my life."

— Kitty Tsui

CHAPTER 6

Wyoming: A Window Into Going to Court

A GRANDFATHER HAD a falling out with his son.

The grandfather had remarried after a divorce from the son's mother. Now that he and his wife were retired they wanted to travel.

The grandchild had reached the age of three around the time his dad and grandpa were battling. The status quo of Grandpa freely visiting his grandson was no longer an option.

Since the grandparents lived in another state and traveled it created inconsistent visitation with the child. The grandparents stayed in touch by phone when away and always remembered birthdays and holidays.

But once the relationship between Dad and Grandpa unraveled, Grandpa found it was becoming difficult to visit the child. When attempts at communication and reconciliation failed, Grandpa sought legal counsel.

The best the grandparents were able to receive by court ruling in the way of access was temporary FaceTime visits with the child, so that meant no more in-person visits. This was certainly better than nothing, and not so unusual in a digital world. During the weekly calls, the child appeared happy and looked like he enjoyed the attention.

I traveled to Wyoming last year as an expert witness in this particular grandparent visitation case. Although it was my first time working in this position, I would do everything possible to fight for the grandparent-grandchild relationship.

The first step was to prepare a lengthy report, which included a selection of previous grandparent cases to cite as examples of the harmful consequences experienced by grandchildren as a result of the separation. A curriculum vitae with my qualifications was also required.

Three months later I was on a plane headed for Casper Wyoming. Since there was no direct flight from John Wayne Airport, in California , I first flew to Denver where I changed planes. I wasn't thrilled with the small commuter jet that I refer to as a tin can because it's so confining and noisy. I ended up in the last row and felt so claustrophobic like the ceiling and walls were closing in on me. Thankfully it was a short 50-minute flight.

Upon landing on the tarmac and exiting down the

mobile stairs, it was just steps to the interior of the tiny two gate airport. Once inside it was a straight shot to the exit to find ground transportation, or so I thought. Standing on the sidewalk in front of the country airport, I didn't see a single cab. Or bus or Uber. Ok, no problem, I pulled up my Lyft app on my phone and reserved a ride. But wait, did I read right? 35 minutes?

Frustrated, I turned and headed back inside to get help with a ride to my hotel. I flagged down a man who was wearing a white neck collar—a good bet he was a pastor. He was literally the only person around, and when I stopped him and inquired about a ride, he said to call Casper Cab, then pointed to the wall across the room where a three foot plastic coated ad hung bearing the phone number.

Dave called me right back after I left a message and said that there was only one cab in service at the moment and it was on its way to the airport to pick up passengers, suggesting I could always ask to share the van with them. When I asked the ETA, he said 20 minutes. Better than 35.

I then noticed a woman sitting on a bench with luggage and decided to ask her how she was getting picked up. It seems she and her husband were the passengers who had booked the cab. I asked her if I could share a ride. She hesitantly agreed, with the condition only if there was room, since they had a ton of luggage.

A few minutes later a dented, scratched and faded red van pulled up with a crusty female driver, who was none to shy about making room for me as an addition to the group. It was, after all more money in her pocket.

I canceled my Lyft and of course got charged a penalty since the driver was apparently already on his way. It didn't matter. I just wanted to get going. In hindsight, maybe I should have waited. Instead of en route to my hotel we were aimed in the opposite direction to drop the couple off only to turn around after getting on the freeway to return his glasses that he left on the seat. Now the 15 to 20 minute drive to my hotel turned into an hour by the time we circled back to the first drop off.

It seemed like forever to get there with the ground transportation delay, time change and well, flying a route that included stops and plane changes. Now I had to find food. My accommodations were labeled an extended stay, I suppose since it had a kitchenette and apparently didn't include daily maid service , which I didn't realize during booking.

I passed on the Denny's conveniently located across the parking lot and opted for a nice long walk to a grocery store up the road. The hotel receptionist was kind enough to give me visual directions that were easy since the landmarks were clusters of one fast food joint after another. "Right behind Wendy's," she said as she pointed in that direction.

Ridley's was a nice big market that was unique to the area, but a bit of a challenging experience to navigate. This ate up more time since I wanted to be back before dark especially in unfamiliar territory. Plus I could only buy what I could carry which meant dinner and breakfast. I wasn't about to cook anything so I opted for the deli and one of those standard baked chicken breasts. I didn't care. I was starving.

The next morning I walked across the parking lot to a Marriott hotel where the two attorneys were staying and attended a meeting they had requested. This was the first time meeting them in person since so far our conversations had been via telephone and mostly email as I was in California and they were in Wyoming.

We sat in a quiet section of the lobby near a back window where we discussed the upcoming case schedule for an hour. Arrangements were made to meet again at 12:30 in order to carpool to court. The lead attorney and associate attorney talked about the case and the respondents' legal council. They informed me that the first order of business was about me. I was stunned. Apparently it's not uncommon for opposing council to dispute expert witnesses and request removing them.

What was going to happen was everyone shows up at the 1:30 court appointed time while the opposing counsel raises the issue to quash my inclusion. If the judge agrees then I'm gone, if not, then I remain in Wyoming until it's my time to testify.

The pretrial motion was presented by the opposing council attorney, who came off as rattled.

In my opinion she didn't offer much in the way of a compelling explanation, and to top it off she seemed confused about scheduling her expert witness and the judge admonished her.

The plaintiff associate attorney, the one I was working for, then presented a sound argument and account of all the reasons why I should stay. The judge was anxious to move on and get the trial started. She allowed me to remain as an expert witness. With that out of the way I, along with anyone else who would be testifying, had to vacate the courtroom until called.

It was hurry up and wait. Don't go too far in case you're called on to testify. Once outside the step-grandmother, other family members, and a friend, who came to offer support as a character witness, all congregated on the patio near the parking lot of the building. I was introduced to everyone and then ended up hopping in the truck of the friend, who was also their banker, to make a coffee run.

The conversation became more relaxed now that everyone was refreshed with beverages. We all watched the clock and after two hours not having been summoned, I called a ride share and said my goodbyes. The attorney indicated that I'd most likely be called the following day since there were others ahead of me and court ended at 5 pm.

The next morning I rode with the attorney again to court and when we arrived I was given the list of questions that the associate attorney would be asking me. There were four pages. I felt like I was cramming for a test without proper time to prepare, and within an unnatural environment that screamed stressful.

I had been relegated to a cramped outer room adjacent to the courtroom where I could pour through the questions. I was about to run to the drinking fountain when suddenly the door flew open and the associate called me into the courtroom. I thought I had more time since the step grandmother was testifying first, which should have taken up more than the ten minutes.

By the time I was sworn in by the female judge and made my way to the witness box, I had no saliva in my mouth. I thought about asking for water but I just wanted to stay focused and not disrupt the proceeding. I should have. I could hardly speak. Not a good way to start off.

The attorney began with a few informational questions about my background and then she deviated from the prep list, which threw me. Some of her questions weren't clear and she ended up withdrawing them. What I found disturbing was that she focused more on my college degree and my major, which had occurred forty years ago. It seemed to be more about credentials than experience. Then she brought me a small tablet computer that played a video of one of the FaceTime visits between Grandpa and Grandson and went on to ask me if I thought the child had been coached. Where did that come from?

I had been the one who requested the grandparent's video so I could be better informed to testify after observing. A couple weeks before the case began, the attorneys decided that they also needed my videos. I was not informed that I would be reviewing them in court and that they would be part of my testimony. Anxiety producing.

After about ten minutes of questioning from the associate attorney, the responding attorney took her shot. Again she seemed unprepared and yes somewhat hostile. Maybe because she didn't prevail on the motion to remove me. Surprisingly her questions were brief. Maybe five minutes or less. Then she closed with asking if I thought all grandparents should have visitation? I didn't see that coming and hopefully recovered when I responded that those with criminal tendencies or are a threat to a child's safety should not. That was it maybe four questions total.

With no further questions in the queue, I was released and high tailed to the facilities and drinking fountain. When I returned to the courtroom, I took a seat in the back row and observed the testimony of the child's mother, who had just taken the stand. She shrugged her shoulders quite a bit and was very matter-of-fact in her dialogue and descriptions.

The judge excused everyone at noon and I said my goodbyes in hopes to catch an earlier flight so I wouldn't have to spend another night. Since the judge would be ruling in 30 days in writing, there was no reason for me to sit through the afternoon session.

There were no more flights from Casper that day,

so I was stuck. I decided a move to a hotel closer to the airport that had a shuttle to the airport would be a good plan. Plus they had a restaurant on site.

The rest of the trip was uneventful until I engaged in conversation with my seatmate on the commuter flight to Denver. He was a local attorney and wanted to know all about my expert witness experience. He asked for my card for someone that he knew who was going through grandparent visitation problems. That's usually the case, someone always knows someone who has been affected.

"Grandma always made you feel she had been waiting to see just you all day and now the day was complete."

— Marcy DeMaree

CHAPTER 7

More About State Laws

IN THE 1970'S states began enacting grandparent visitation laws as a result of the escalation of family estrangement, often involving grandparents. Today all 50 states have some type of grandparent visitation law. These laws, however do not give grandparents the absolute right to visitation as previously mentioned.

Each of the 50 states' grandparent visitation statutes specifies circumstances under which grandparents have standing to petition for court-ordered visitation. Parental fundamental rights are affected by these laws, which means the courts have subjected them to a strict scrutiny standard. The due process and equal protection requirements of the Fourteenth Amendment have also been applied. In the pivotal case on grandparents' visitation rights, Troxel v. Granville, the U.S. Supreme Court (2000) found the

State of Washington's grandparent visitation statute unconstitutional and invalid. The Court ruled that the law's interference with the parent's right to make decisions concerning the care, custody, and control of her daughters violated the Due Process Clause.

CALIFORNIA

Under California law, the court can grant a grandparent reasonable visitation with a grandchild, but only under certain circumstances. Family Codes 3100-3105.

California law allows the court to grant reasonable visitation to a grandparent when the court finds:

a. There is a preexisting relationship between grandparent and grandchild that "has engendered a bond," such that visitation is in the best interest of the child, and
b. The best interests of the child in having visitation with a grandparent are balanced against the rights of the parents to make decisions about their child.

In general, grandparents cannot file for visitation rights while the grandchild's parents are married with the following exceptions:

a. The parents are living separately and apart on a permanent or indefinite basis
b. A parent's whereabouts are unknown (and have been for at least a month)
c. One of the parents joins the grandparent's petition for visitation

d. The child does not live with either of his or her parents
e. The grandchild has been adopted by a stepparent, or
f. One of the parents is incarcerated or voluntarily institutionalized.

California has a strong policy preference for the rights of parents over non-parents. Under California law there is a rebuttable presumption against grandparent visitation where the child's parents agree the grandparent should not be granted visitation rights or if the parents are not united in their opposition, but grandparent visitation is contested by the custodial parent.

To start a request for visitation with a grandchild through the court, the grandparent must know if there is a case open between the parents. If there is an open case, such as a divorce or parentage case, most likely the Grandparent will need to file a Joinder and Request for Order to obtain a court date. If there is no case filed between the parents, the grandparent will need to file a new case by creating their own unique Petition and Request for Order.

CONNECTICUT SEC. 46-B-59

In Connecticut, grandparents have the right to petition the court for visitation rights. When a grandparent seeks visitation, they must show that the relationship between them and the child is similar to a parent-child relationship and that the denial of visitation would cause real and significant harm to the child.

According to DivorceNet, Grandparents are entitled to broad legal protections in Connecticut. While parents and grandparents aren't equal under the law, grandparents do have unique privileges. Specifically, grandparents can petition (request) visitation when the following factors are present:

- a parent-like relationship exists between the grandparent and grandchild, and
- a denial of visitation would significantly harm the child.

In one Connecticut case, a father restricted visits with the maternal grandmother after the children's mother committed suicide. The grandmother requested visitation over the father's objection. Prior to the mother's death, the grandmother visited the children several times a week and regularly babysat, cooked, and cared for the children. However, the grandmother lost her request because she didn't demonstrate that she had assumed parenting responsibilities or that the children would be harmed if they stopped seeing her.

A judge must balance grandparent visitation with the parent-child relationship. A parent's time with a child comes first, so grandparent visitation cannot unreasonably interfere with the parent-child relationship.

WYOMING 20-7-101
Establishing grandparents' visitation rights.

> (a) A grandparent may bring an original action against any person having custody of the grandparent's minor grandchild to establish reasonable visitation rights to the child. If the court finds, after a hearing, that visitation would be in the best interest of the child and that the rights of the child's parents are not substantially impaired, the court shall grant reasonable visitation rights to the grandparent. In any action under this section for which the court appoints a guardian ad litem, the grandparent shall be responsible for all fees and expenses associated with the appointment.

It's worth noting that WRAB Law firm located in Cheyenne, Wyoming published an update on their website regarding a recent grandparent case.

THE WYOMING SUPREME COURT OVERHAULS GRANDPARENTS' RIGHTS
Grandparents' visitation rights is a relatively new area of Wyoming law. Originally as common law, grandparents had no right to visitation with their grandchildren without consent from the children's parents. However, in 1991 the Wyoming Legislature adopted Wyoming Statute 20-7-101, which allowed

grandparents to seek visitation rights to their grandchildren in court. Wyoming courts often state that the Wyoming Legislature transformed grandparent visitation rights from a moral obligation to a legal obligation when it adopted the grandparent rights statute.

The grandparent rights statute has gone through significant revisions throughout the years. The statute required that the grandparents show that visitation would be in the best interests of the child and that the parents' rights would not be substantially impaired by allowing the grandparents to have visitation with the children.

The Wyoming Supreme Court has radically changed the way courts must handle grandparent visitation cases. In the 2022 case, Ailport v. Ailport, the Wyoming Supreme Court drew a clear line in the parents' favor in grandparent visitation cases. In Ailport, the grandparents sought visitation with their five grandchildren. The District Court ruled that the grandparents did not prove their right to visitation (i.e. that visitation was in the best interests of the children and would not substantially impair the parents' rights). The grandparents appealed the case to the Wyoming Supreme Court.

The Wyoming Supreme Court agreed with the District Court, but used a different analysis to get to that result. The Wyoming Supreme Court focused on the fundamental constitutional right of parents to raise their children as the parents saw fit. The Wyoming Supreme Court held that the way judges were interpreting the grandparent rights statute failed to adequately account for the parents' constitutional rights. The Wyoming Supreme Court held:

> Parents have a fundamental due process right to guide the upbringing of their children, including determining the level of contact with their grandparents. To satisfy strict scrutiny, [the grandparent rights statute] must be interpreted to protect parents' fundamental right by requiring grandparents to prove parents are unfit to make visitation decisions for their children or the parents' visitation decisions are or will be harmful to the children. Only after the grandparents make that threshold showing by clear and convincing evidence may the district court determine what visitation is in the best interests of the children.

FLORIDA

According to the The Florida Bar Newsletter, Gov. Ron DeSantis has signed a measure that expands a grandparent's right to petition for visitation, but only in tragic circumstances.

DeSantis signed HB 1119 by Rep. Jackie Toledo, R-Tampa, on June 24, 2022.

The measure would create a rebuttable presumption for grandparent or step-grandparent visitation, but only in cases where one parent has been found criminally liable for the death of the other parent, or "civilly liable for an intentional tort causing the death" of the other parent. The presumption could only be overcome if the court finds that it is not in the best interest of the child.

Supporters dubbed the measure the "Markel Act." Popular FSU Law Prof. Dan Markel was shot to death in the driveway of his Tallahassee home in 2014. Markel's parents championed grandparent rights after their son's death and supported the measure.

Before DeSantis signed the measure, grandparents in Florida had few legal options. They could seek visitation only when both parents are deceased, missing, or in a "permanent vegetative state," or if the other parent has been convicted of a violent felony. Even then, the petitioner must establish that the surviving parent is unfit and poses a significant risk to the child.

In 2020, Sen. Jeff Brandes, R-St. Petersburg, sponsored similar legislation, SB 1886. It died in the Judiciary Committee.

The latest version enjoyed enthusiastic bipartisan support. Senate Democratic Leader Lauren Book of Ft. Lauderdale thanked Sen. Keith Perry, R-Gainesville, for sponsoring the companion, SB 1408. "It's going to be a wonderful thing for families across the state of Florida," Book said.

Sen. Dennis Baxley, R-Lady Lake, quipped earlier this year, "this is the best thing that we've got going all session. At the end of the day, many of us got more character development from our grandparents than any other person," he said.

The WFSU Public Media wrote that the Florida courts have consistently found that statutes based solely on "best interest of the child" when attempting to compel grandparent visitation are unconstitutional. The rulings acknowledge the fundamental right to parent without intrusion by the government has long been recognized by the United States and Florida constitutions.

"A lot of people nowadays have their children raised by the grandparents. It's not uncommon for that to happen, and there are many, many situations where the grandparents have had the children for many years," said Rep. Michelle Salzman, R-Pensacola. "Then the parent comes back from either incarceration, or they've just decided that they're ready to take their children, and they can take them back without any visitation, without allowing those grandparents to see those children ever again."

Salzman says the bill "does not create an umbrella protection for grandparents to stay engaged in the grandchildren's lives," but she calls it "a great step forward."

"As a father of 5 and a grandfather of 8, I take this very personal," said Sen. Dennis Baxley, R-Ocala.

"I am extremely pleased to see us look out for the wellness of these children and the opportunity for these relationships to be nourished no matter what shape families are in. They need to see their granddad once in a while."

CHAPTER 8

Why We Need Advocacy

PART OF BEING an advocate for children's rights is giving them a voice about whom they may love. And since children do not have a voice or choice, it's up to the grandparents to speak for them. One way to be an advocate for grandparent rights is to ensure that they continue to maintain a relationship with their grandchildren. Our advocacy that supports the grandparent-grandchild connection is the creation of the 2005 nonprofit charitable organization, ADVOCATES FOR GRANDPARENT GRANDCHILD CONNECTION, of which I am the founder.

In my first book, *GRAND WISHES,* I defined the **what** about the issue and went on to describe the *why* of the vital grandparent grandchild relationship.

In my second book, *A PRECIOUS BOND,* I guided disenfranchised grandparents toward the **how** to maintain that relationship.

In my third grandparent book, *GRAND DISTANCE,* I revealed the **where** describing what I chose to do to hold onto my grandchild, creating a nontraditional relationship.

It's no wonder grandparents have become reluctant to file petitions for visitation. The diverse laws and ever changing and challenging hoops that they have to jump through, along with financial burden, add up. The "harm" criteria, which have either been adopted by state codes or are a result of a ruling causing the setting of a new precedent, are tough. This hurdle can be difficult to overcome because the harm isn't necessarily immediately visible. If grandparents have been kept away, they aren't able to witness the child's behavior. All they can communicate is historical instances when the child demonstrated obvious, blatant behavior about wanting to spend time with grandparents. And parents certainly aren't going to provide that information in order to assist the grandparent case. Grandparents therefore, become intimidated and give up when they hear they have to prove harm. Without access, visual proof or a court appointed psychologist to observe the child's emotional distress, there's little hope.

The only way to validate the harm is to observe the grandchild as discussed in chapter 4. When grandparents are in touch with grandchildren during the litigation process, for example, they are more apt to glean nuggets of information from the child. The child may be upset because they think Grandma has forgotten them, or blame themselves for lack of visits, thinking they did something wrong. Their emotional state is fragile and distress can cause depression. So unless the child is older and can communicate their wishes, it pretty much is in the hands of a professional therapist to determine the degree of harm, if any.

Those grandparents who are granted some sort of temporary visitation during an ongoing legal battle where they are able to determine the child's emotional state would still be required to prove harm in a court of law.

Grandparents in a non legal situation where they are forced to comply with the parents' demands for limited access pretty much have to tolerate the status quo rather than seek legal avenues. Otherwise they risk losing complete access. The best they can do is provide a balance by being there for the child, no matter how infrequent.

With no access, it's when the child is eighteen or older or when the grandparents are able to see the child they learn after the fact what the child experienced. The more access grandparents have to the grandchild the better to observe the child's behavior and not only be there as a vital support system in their life, but also gather information.

For example during a court case where visitation is limited, a child's emotions can fluctuate due to the change in circumstances. The child senses the strain between parents and grandparents. Even without an ongoing court case kids have a keen sense of awareness when the status quo is off and has been disrupted. So, when there is an apparent rift between parents and grandparents where there may be increased parental control over visitation access, the child will behave differently. Differently, and not in a good way, when their loving grandparent's time with them is suddenly altered.

Kids pick up on everything even when they are supposedly kept out of adult conversations. Obviously, when visits change a child will notice. They don't have to witness an incident to know things are different. The weekend overnights may be eliminated, going to Grandma's house may no longer happen. Now Grandma comes to their house and only when Mom or Dad is home.

How can this not affect the child's feelings? Children need structure and some sort of consistency, even if the consistency means an inconsistent schedule due to long distance. The consistency comes in the knowing that grandparents will be coming back. Children need love and affection continually. Children need to feel loved at all times which requires constant reinforcement from the people in their lives. Specifically parents, grandparents, significant adults with whom they have established a bond.

Sure, things happen, people get sick, have emergencies, travel but these are most often temporary setbacks, inconveniences. And children should be taught to understand when Grandma took a cruise or broke her leg. They need to be a part of the conversation so that they can learn to adapt to change. But sudden unexplained change or change covered by lies is when the child becomes anxious, confused, upset.

Not quite the same as a close family member, but an additional source of information about a child's behavior and emotional state would be a professional child psychologist. Teachers, coaches, anyone who has a relationship with the child can also be a good observer of a child's behavior.

"Grandparents are like stars. You don't always see them, but you know they're there."

— Unknown

CHAPTER 9

Quality verses Quantity

IS THERE A formula for how many hours a grandparent is supposed to spend with grandkids? Is there a recommended daily requirement that should be followed?

Apparently this is a subject that arises during court cases. This is the case in certain states that have adopted a code requiring grandparents to have a parentlike relationship with the child before they can petition the court for visitation. While there are some grandparents who have had to assume the responsibility of raising their grandchild, most do not have the title of full time custodial caregiver. Instead they are considered an extended family member, a family loved one. Everyone plays a role in a child's life. All valuable. The village and all that.

The laws are all over the place because they are not

federal but state specific.

I wish that there were a federal statute that would protect children's rights to maintain a relationship with a grandparent. It shouldn't be that hard to be allowed to love someone. But time after time kids are treated like property. Over and over again their voices are non-existent. I repeat: NO VOICE NO CHOICE.

When parents get so wrapped up in the anger it becomes more important than the child's feelings. They love the anger. I think that's it. They become focused on anger and retaliation kicks in, overriding the child's feelings. These parents don't possess the wisdom that comes with life experience. These parents don't have the capacity to step outside themselves and consider another's feelings. They cannot step into someone else's shoes because these parents are "ME" focused.

Grandparents become so desperate they trot into court right off the bat without taking a breath and analyzing the consequences. Once the parents are served with papers, it causes the relationship to fail, which only increases anger and puts up an even bigger wall. In most cases there is now no turning back leaving no room for negotiation, diplomacy, reconciliation, compromise. The battle is on; everyone is now in fighting mode rather than communication mode.

Why is communication so hard? Have they not been taught how to do this? For generations, we were brought up to keep our feelings and emotions to ourselves, I suppose that's part of it. People just didn't talk about it. Are we so programmed to hold everything inside?

As a result of taking the legal route the grandparents become alienated and are cutoff from visiting grandkids. By the time they retain council, file the petition and get a court date months have gone by without seeing the child. Continuances, mediation, motions, depositions all delay access.

When a grandparent lives out of state or even in another country, are they considered less important? Can a child still have a loving relationship with a grandparent who isn't physically close by? What about FaceTime, telephone calls, or Skype? There are ways to connect when distance prevents in-person contact.

It seems the focus is on quantity when a statute demands there must be a parent-like relationship between the grandparent and the child, and prove that denial of visitation would cause real and significant harm.

These are impossible hurdles to overcome for a grandparent. They are unrealistic. Some grandparents actually are engaged in a parent-like role—maybe they live with the child and their parent or, in some cases grandparents have had to assume the custodial caretaker role when a parent is absent, such as incarcerated or loss of custody. The majority of grandparents, however do not have the parent-like relationship. They don't want to be the parent, they don't want to discipline or raise the grandchild;

they've already done that. They simply want to provide a mix of love and affection to the child. They want to spend quality time with the child. Grandma and Grandpa most likely are retired and may now travel so they aren't always close by the grandchild. This does not necessarily mean they no longer have a relationship with their grandchild. It's just different. Who says relationships can only happen if you have close proximity? Families are scattered these days and aren't necessarily dependent on grandparents as caregivers.

Besides traveling, retired grandparents often engage in leisure activities, sports, classes all things they didn't have time to do when raising their own children.

Sadly this could be held against grandparents in a court of law. During a grandparent visitation case a parent may raise the issue of the grandparents not being around consistently because they frequently travel. Grandparents may have a second home where they divide their time. Lets not forget the grandparents that also work at jobs. Do they get a pass?

As ridiculous as this sounds judges have been known to consider the amount of time—*quantity*—during the decision making process of arriving at a ruling. So less time = negative. More time = positive. *Quality* isn't a barometer during the decision making process.

Why is it a competition between quality and quantity? It makes no sense. It's a narrow-minded assumption, as is the criteria of parent-like role. In other words the more time spent with the child the more important the relationship. I guess that means grandparents need to live under the same roof in order to secure the relationship from future estrangement? But wait, I've seen that one lose in court as well.

"Grandmas and grandpas are grand-angels."

— Terri Guillemets

CHAPTER 10

Boundaries

WE ALL KNOW grandparents are notorious for spoiling grandchildren. They mean well, but sometimes they overstep boundaries. Grandparents can have the mindset that they somehow need to compensate for mistakes they made as parents by over indulging the grandkids. They want to give a little more now that they have more time, wisdom and money. But those good intentions aren't always well received. The parents are steering the ship and all decisions are theirs to make when it comes to their child.

Before grandparents make plans, check with Mom and Dad. In other words making assumptions that it's ok to make reservations for travel or activities without parental consent is probably not a good idea. Before grandparents make extravagant purchases or buy anything that may be out of the norm, the parents should be consulted. It's not uncommon for gifts to be returned by refusing to accept. I hear this all the time and it also happened to me. The big yellow pedal car that I delivered as a birthday gift I found sitting on my front patio the next morning when I opened the door to retrieve the paper.

"It's Easier to Ask Forgiveness Than It Is To Get Permission." (Rear Admiral Grace Hopper, U.S. Navy). Nope, this does not work here. It's always better to ask first no matter how insignificant it may seem to the grandparents. Parental control must be respected.

A grandmother, had asked her daughter-in-law about an upcoming open house at her granddaughter's school and the DIL had said she'd let her know. A couple of weeks went by and when the grandmother didn't hear from her, she stopped by the school to get the dates. All hell broke lose. The grandmother had nothing to hide so she mentioned to the DIL that she got the schedule and would be there. It seems like an innocent thing to do, but the DIL didn't think so and perceived it as disrespect. "What, now you don't trust me to give you the information?" Grandma was stunned. She apologized and defended her actions, but Mom was still pissed off.

Another boundary issue is giving advice freely and without solicitation. And that's a big one. Being a grandparent does not entitle you to run the show. Even if you see parents making the wrong decision, butt out and bite your tongue. Step aside and let the parents stumble or not, it's not your call.

Those who cannot help themselves and have to chime in will regret it. It's not who has the most experience that gets to make the decision, or who is the wisest, right or wrong, it's the parents. They are in charge. Always.

Offering up unsolicited advice is a stumbling stone. It could cost the grandparents and ultimately the child dearly. It could be the cause of estrangement.

This is a big one and grandparents need to learn to keep their opinions to themselves. They could say the wrong thing once and be cut off. Or for those parents who have more patience, after repeated interference from the grandparent, they may finally call for a time out.

It's best not to give help until asked. Keep it to yourself and let the parents figure it out for themselves. They resent the suggestions and will take them personally as a slight against them. It comes across as saying that they aren't able or capable. Kind of like how the message that the grandmother who went to the school was perceived by the DIL. Even though this wasn't about giving advice or opinion, the DIL took it as not being able or capable of doing the task. It doesn't matter what the grandparents' intention is, it still sounds like a criticism.

And when you're asked for advice and opinions, tread lightly. Avoid, 'I think you should,' 'well, you may want to...' 'The best way to do this or that.'

Instead turn it around, "hmm, I'm not sure, what

do you think?" Or "let me think about that." "All I can say is this or that has worked for me..." There are ways of offering support without bulldozing.

Another example of overstepping boundaries is expectations. In other words, seeing the child on your terms. Grandparents get carried away and forget that grandchildren are not theirs to visit whenever they feel like it. Dropping by unannounced may not be such a good idea unless there happens to be an agreement in place.

Telling the parents when they want to visit rather than asking, does not go over well. When a grandparent starts placing demands on the parents about spending time with the child, it puts up the parent's defenses. Asking is fine, along with accepting the answer without argument if it isn't what you want to hear. No arguing.

A communication technique is to ask, respond with acceptance, and then ask when is a good time? If you receive a noncommittal answer, for example, offer an option: "how about eight or or nine?". Or "How about next Tuesday or Wednesday; does that work for you?"

If you still don't get a commitment, then let it go and take a break for week or so. Parents need space and don't like being put on the spot. Give them some room.

When there is a less than amicable relationship between parents and grandparents there are solutions. I have had cases where the grandparent pulls up to the curb to pick up kids and have their visit away from the home. This has occurred when the grandparent and the parent are in a strained relationship yet one or both of the parents figured out that just because they don't get along, the child shouldn't be estranged from grandparents.

Grandparents have become so incensed about not having visits go their way, whether time or place, that they have taken the legal route thinking a court order would provide them more access. That is simply wrong. If parents offer any kind of visits, and the grandparents aren't happy and want more, they will very well lose what they once had. If you have any kind of visits, be grateful.

Grandparents fill a gap and kids feel good about themselves when they are loved. Children have their needs met when there is a balance in their life that Grandparents provide. Remember how important you are and do everything you possibly can to ensure that you keep your foot in the door.

"Grandchildren give us a second chance to do things better because they bring out the best in us.

—Unknown

CHAPTER 11

Reasons to deny

MONEY.
Grandparents are sometimes expected to freely provide financial support to their grown children. And when they don't, they may be cut off. The parents probably are part of the "me" generation and feel a sense of entitlement.

If the parent is struggling and sees the grandparents living comfortably they are of the belief that they deserve part of the pot. Maybe they need help with a new car or down payment on a house. When they go to Dad and ask for financial assistance and it's not forthcoming the pushback begins. They are accustomed to getting what they want from their parents. They have never before been denied and when they are, they can't understand. They can't accept it either. The parents come to realize that they are enabling the adult child by not putting their foot down and that's when the grandchild becomes the pawn.

OPPORTUNITY

Believe it or not, some parents and yes, some people in general, are looking for opportunities to become offended. It's a form of pessimism, negativity. They aren't the ones who look on the bright side. Instead they look on the dark side. They look for reasons to criticize.

Apparently they get some sort of payoff for being critical. Just like everyone else, we all behave in ways that are rewarded. We do the things we do because there's a payoff. Maybe these negative folks are happy being negative? Or fulfilled by being angry? By constantly looking for reasons to be offended they can fulfill themselves by bitching, complaining, criticizing, and getting pissed off at others. It's a way of life. Human behavior.

OVERSTEPPING BOUNDARIES

This behavior covers a lot of territory as discussed in Chapter 10, and it's a big one for denial. An overstep could be the examples cited in the previous chapter along with basically anything the parent perceives as an overstep. If the parent believes it to be so, then it is. Giving unsolicited advice. It could be once, or it could be frequent. With some parents it takes only one instance. Others are more tolerant and may reach their boiling point if grandparents have gotten away with too freely given advice too long and pushed them too far. Getting bossy toward parents happens a lot and is never acceptable. No one appreciates being told what to do. Butting in rather minding your own business, never a good thing. Making decisions unilaterally that includes a child without consulting parent. The list goes on.

DISAGREEMENTS

Differences of opinion will always be an issue that crosses all subjects.

Yes, even a so-called friendly political debate can sever relationships. Discussions get out of control and become arguments. Political or otherwise. Families have become fractured over political opinions that have been shared. Nowadays more than ever. It seems there's no such thing as constructive criticism or a healthy debate anymore.

LITIGATION

Grandparents can jump the gun before trying to work things out and think by filing a petition for court ordered visitation will get them access and instead does the opposite, especially when they don't follow through. Filing a petition, serving the parent and then withdrawing prior to completion is a sure way to provoke the parents into a permanent state of hostility.

Or filing a petition, serving the parent, seeing the process through with mediation, a hearing and in some cases a trial, will drive a wedge like no other. This may get you court ordered consistently scheduled visits, which would be a success for you and the child. The parent will be angry for a very long time—maybe forever over the control that they lost.

The anger in some cases escalates into a sabotage of visits. Winning a case in court does not necessarily mean a guarantee of enforcement. The excuses are subtle and can be a passive aggressive behavior; either way some parents will do whatever it takes to impede the visits. The kid is sick, he didn't want to go, we forgot, out of town, family emergency and on and on.

There have been cases when parents are so hell bent on winning, they move. Anything to make it harder on the grandparent. And not just from one city to another but sometimes out of state. If grandparents can afford it, they find a new attorney in the area where the child resides. With an order in place, it's a matter of transferring the case. Depending on the state, it may be difficult to exercise visitation rights when an order is in place in a different state, something an attorney would be the best resource for advice.

In our experience, we have found that grandparents who take the least adversarial approach are the ones who have the best success rates of remaining connected. Communication is the key, yet it's the least used solution. Individuals get hung up on egos and the need to be right.

There is an abundance of professional resources available to assist. Finding a neutral third party intervention, talk therapy, instruction, books, or mediation—all are a benefit toward opening communication. I know the family law courts require mediation, but by the time both parties get there it's often too late and the walls go up and prevent any progress.

DEATH

When I first started this organization death of a parent seemed a rare criteria for denied grandparent visitation, or at least I hadn't experienced the issue. But no longer.

When one of the parents dies, the surviving spouse has been known to distance themselves from the parents of the deceased spouse. More common is when the parents had been separated or divorced. But when they are married and living in an intact household it still happens. Unbelievable.

In Carmen's situation this occurred after her daughter passed away from an illness. Almost the same scenario occurred in California, when Grandmother Judy's daughter was killed by a drunk driver. In both cases the parents had been divorced. In Judy's case, the dad moved to Washington state, where the grandparent laws were less friendly and completely cut off the grandparents. The two children grew up without access to their maternal grandparents, aunts, uncles and cousins.

Two other California grandmothers who both happen to live on Balboa Island, lost their sons who had both been married and living in an intact household when they died. In each case the daughter-in-law suddenly pulled away. There wasn't much in the way of a disagreement; it was more an obvious campaign to distance themselves from Grandma.

Death of a parent being part of many state codes can also provide standing to file a petition for visitation in court. Once again it depends on the state.

DIVORCE

Divorce is also a part of many state codes that provides standing for grandparents to file. However, it like death can also be another situation where grandparents get cast aside. Everyone takes sides and the dividing line becomes clear. Even though Grandparents do their best to remain neutral for the child's sake, it's a difficult task to accomplish.

Maybe one of the parents is emotionally distraught, unstable, uninvolved, causing the grandparents to have difficulty keeping involved with the child. Sometimes the other parent who is the in-law doesn't like the parent and uses their access as a bargaining chip while embroiled in dissolution negotiations.

CHAPTER 12

Going to Court

MAKING THE DECISION to file a petition for visitation requires much thought and planning and should not be done hastily.

Consulting a family law attorney with grandparent visitation cases is a must. Consulting an attorney who is familiar with the courthouse that has jurisdiction also a must. Knowing the judges and opposing counsel can only be an advantage.

Consulting an attorney who explains the pros and cons of litigation is one who is looking out for your best interest and not there own.

A good way to find an attorney other than word of mouth is to do your shopping in the courthouse. Make a trip to the court and observe. Go inside the courtroom and observe the attorneys in action. Observe the judges, the entire procedure. Not only will this help to find representation but seeing the process will alleviate anxiety of the unknown. Spend time in the hallways, and lobby, talk to clients, talk to attorneys, talk to clerks, talk to bailiffs. Familiarize your self with the environment. Just like you would with any other new experience.

Going to court is not for the faint of heart. It's daunting. It's scary especially when the case escalates to a trial. Intimidating.

Beginning the process by filing a petition is a time consuming endeavor. It could be more than a year. The longer it goes on the longer it will be before you see your grandchild. However, if there's absolutely no other way to work it out and you have done everything possible to take the least adversarial approach, and if you have nothing to lose by embarking on a court battle then you'll have to put in the time. Some judges will, however rule on behalf of the grandparent by giving them temporary visitation. Again, a sharp attorney will request such action.

Let's say you win your case, which will also deepen the anger and hostility of the parents, which could thwart occasional visits. So now were talking about enforcement.

Obtaining court ordered visitation is one thing but enforcing is another. Excuses such as: "he's sick, she has a doctor appointment, we're out of town" can be used.

During a temporary visitation agreement, the parents went so far as to put the child up to saying on tape that he didn't want to talk to Grandpa.

Then there's the issue of not finishing what you start. Grandparents jump in and realize that they have made the wrong decision for various reasons. They see how the child ends up in the middle and sense the stress that has been put upon them being tugged in two different directions. There is a degree of brain washing that occurs when the parents begin to bad mouth the grandparents. The child doesn't know what to believe. When they are in the presence of the grandparent they may withdraw as a result of the brainwashing. I refer to this grandparent alienation condition as GAS (grandparent alienation syndrome) as opposed to PAS (parent alienation syndrome).

Another reason for stopping the process is funds. It can get expensive. And risky as there are no guarantees. Maybe a 50/50 chance, maybe less for the grandparents?

Grandparents sometimes stop everything because they have had a change of heart. Maybe after thinking it over they realize it is costing everyone, financially and emotionally. Maybe seeing the parents stretch their income to fight at the risk of taking something away from the kid? Maybe the grandparents realize if they lose it truly is over and there will never be a reconciliation. Which brings me to the point of no return. Once you file a petition and put the parents on notice there is no going back. Even after you cancel.

AS a grandparent, referred to it as "power pills" for

the parents. They have always had the power to raise the child as they see fit. But now the power extends to future relationships with grandparents that have now been tainted. They will be punished for what they did. No forgiveness. No moving on.

The parents will tell the grandparents, "we need time to heal." "We need to regain trust." They are the victims, they are the ones who have been wronged and they will never let the grandparents forget that.

Grandparent, Carol Menck said, "I feel like the laws make it near impossible for the grandparents. Somehow, parents should not be allowed to use the children to punish us the way they can now. Maybe if that were changed to be seen as a form of emotional child abuse.

"I don't know...then maybe parents wouldn't find it so easy to do. Then they might be able to work it out in the family without going to court...automatically ordered to family therapy with an impartial therapist who specializes in this.

"So much is wrong with the court; games are allowed to be played, parents (and some grandparents) get away with making up horrible lies. How does that even happen? We are in fear of angering the judge. Most of this isn't even expected by the grandparents."

CHAPTER 13

My Case

I ACTUALLY WENT to court four times.

The first time was with my son, who after two years decided to see his child for the first time. I had been in Jacob's life since he was three days old, my son had not. The visiting, babysitting and even clothing him with children's wear from the retail store I owned, contributed to a precious bond. Everyone was happy and getting along. Until court.

So when I say my son decided, that's not quite true. While I didn't hold a gun to his head, I did encourage him to get involved. He was the missing link. I think he was confused about what he really wanted and about how to get there and was still lagging in maturity. He was only a few years out of high school, so how mature could he have been anyway?

I believe his decision to step up had to do with doing

the right thing. Since the mom refused him access after so long, she held her ground. She was angry that he'd rejected her and then his child as well.

We found an attorney, filed the petition and jumped into the system. First was the mediation, which as I recollect was done in separate rooms—so much for communication. Then there was the hearing and since nothing was resolved a trial was the next step.

In between the filing and the trial, needless to say, my relationship with the mom took a not so friendly turn. Now I was the bad guy for joining in my son's request to visitation. It was really too bad that our relationship could have been so fragile to suddenly be threatened over the fact that the biological father wanted to step forward and be a part of his child's life.

In my observation, the child's father was conflicted but managed to come to his senses. Okay, maybe not at first and maybe he needed a nudge, but truly it shouldn't matter how he got there, but here he was and she's so angry that she is going to deny her child love. All the consoling, persuasion, convincing didn't make a dent. She just needed to cool down. I hoped that she'd come around.

So off we go to court. It was hard seeing my son on the stand and being questioned. Such a foreign experience. His voice was shaky and he stammered. When he took responsibility by admitting to the judge that he made a mistake and was sorry for waiting so long, it was a sign of growth.

As it turns out it was a commissioner who exercised the same power and duties of a judge, who presided over the case. She was a young woman, reminded me of the "Judging Amy" character from a TV show, professional and fair. She ruled in favor of my son, since he was after all, the father. She assigned a 12-week step-up program that began with my son alone in Jacob's home, then I joined, then the last four weeks were away visits.

The mom went ballistic once we exited the courtroom as the two attorneys tried hammering out a visitation schedule. My son's attorney's words will forever be embedded in my memory. He pulled me aside and whispered, "You may want to file for grandparent rights."

I looked at him like he was crazy, and said, "She would never keep me away from Jacob."

The visits lasted about six months before my son threw in the towel. He stopped making the two-hour drive from San Diego after too many confrontations. Since there was no room for error of any kind, he gave up. Then the campaign began for him to give up his rights so the new husband/ stepdad could adopt.

My visits continued, however less frequent. Most visits took place in Jacob's room away from the mom or outside. She never spoke to me, now leaving it up to the stepdad to be the intermediary.

I filed for court ordered visitation and then had second thoughts after a deposition took place and I saw the toll it was taking on all of us. That's when I put an end to it. I apologized, groveled, did everything to make it up. Finally they allowed me sporadic visits and continued to campaign for adoption. Just before Jacob's baby brother was born, the parents informed me they needed a break from visits and cut me off again.

Back to court I went, now with a new attorney, who stated that he was an expert in grandparent visitation. (He made sure I knew he had big name clients to prove it.) Once again a trial, only after the mom reneged on a settlement agreement. The judge refused to rule on behalf of a court ordered visitation order, instead instituting oral instructions that I was to continue to have access to my grandson thereby enacting a Minute Order. The Minute Order read that the parents were to provide monthly visits between Jacob and me and if not she wanted to see them back in her courtroom.

In the mean time, my son, gave up his rights. And even though the parents promised I could continue to visit, I felt that my visits were now numbered. The law states that there is a one year waiting period before the child can be legally adopted.

The visits were once per month for two hours always supervised and always outside or occasionally in his room if it was raining. Toward the end of the year, the visits dwindled. Two months before the year long waiting period the excuses increased and the visits stopped.

In August I got the letter that stated I was no longer allowed to see Jacob.

The law was on their side as California code did not have provisions for grandparents to continue visitation following a stepparent adoption. Meaning, grandparents were no longer recognized. No rights. Period. Along with a biological parent signing off rights, grandparents were wiped out as well.

It took me four years of legislating but I finally persevered thanks to Assemblyman Van Tran and a supportive California legislature at the time. The law that I proposed and ended up sponsoring would now fill that gap by continuing to allow biological grandparents to be a part of the grandchild's life following a stepparent adoption.

A lot happened leading up to the enactment of my law. The adoptive dad contacted me and informed that he and Jacob's mom were divorcing and now he wanted me back in Jacob's life. Of course I jumped at the chance. Jacob was now eight. And it all worked out for about six months with the mom fighting every step of the way to keep me away. A grudge. It got ugly and I was pulled in opposite directions by both parents.

Shortly after the enactment of my law, I hired my third attorney to now file for visitation under my new law. We were so proud to be the first to use the law. The adoptive dad even attended my hearing and supported my case. But then the judge, who hadn't kept current on the new laws that year refused to hear my case. Sheryl Edgar, my attorney, agreed that my civil rights were violated by the judge. We had long talks afterwards, where she observed that I had been through enough. Did I really want to hire another attorney to file a civil rights case? "Go to Italy, live your life," was her advice.

Meanwhile the visits with Jacob continued to be in jeopardy of ending because of the contentious divorce between the parents. The parents' attorneys had recommended that I pause the visits until after the divorce proceedings were complete. The last time I saw Jacob was on Father's Day at Balboa beach. When I hugged him good-bye, I knew that was it.

It ended badly. The dad did a 180 and sided with the mom in a written agreement attached to their divorce settlement that I would be kept from Jacob.

How did I find out? I went to the clerk's office of the family law court in Orange California and looked up their case on my own. No one had the guts to inform me.

As I have shared before I never stopped seeing Jacob. But he did stop seeing me. I reveal in my book, Grand Distance, exactly how I went about becoming an undercover grandma in order to watch my grandson grow up. It was never easy, but most things worthwhile are not.

When he was fourteen, I was allowed back into his life by the adoptive father. It was risky for him but also the right thing to do, sadly it had taken him five years to figure it out. Now the reunification was a challenge since Jacob was no longer a child but a teenager. Sure I saw him from a distance, and even within reach a few times. I always felt happy to have been able to at least see him. I always felt sad that I couldn't interact and let him know that I loved him and had never stopped missing him. I always felt sad wondering what he was thinking when I first disappeared? Not one day went by that I didn't think about him. I wanted to hug him, I wanted to be able to touch him, kiss him, show affection.

The saddest thing of all is that he didn't know any of this. He missed hearing how much I loved him, he missed hearing the praises, the joy that comes from spending time with a grandchild. He missed hearing stories. He missed the affection, the hugs, the kisses, the touch from a loving adult. We had to start over and we are still repairing the damage that the absence caused.

Think about it, five years in a child's life is huge. Especially when they cross from elementary into the teen years and experience all the changes that occur during that transition from childhood to adolescence. The last thing a teenager wants to do is to hang around their grandma. This was a major obstacle to overcome.

Today Jacob is a fine young man. He is kind, focused and responsible. I'm truly proud of him.

The point is we all have to determine what our comfort zone is when dealing with animosity within a family. Our job is to either accept the conditions and go along to get along, or to tolerate ,which could mean going along with rules that are against our better judgment and being miserable. Or waiting until the child turns 18 and becomes an adult to see them—also against our judgment, also being miserable. Or we can by walk away with regret, do nothing and never truly move on with one's life. The pain can be so overwhelming that Grandparents often become numb to the point that they do nothing.

Those who reject the conditions, take action. They go to court hoping to obtain court ordered visitation. They go rogue, like I did and sneak around in the shadows hoping for a glimpse of the kid. Finally they put forth the effort to learn new skills that will teach them how to reconnect with the angry parents. It takes a lot of work to get their foot back in the door. And even if they don't, doing something is better than doing nothing.

What all grandparents must learn is that the parents are not going to change their behavior. I'll say it again the parents are not going to change. The only person to change behavior is yourself. Grandparents can only control their own behavior. A lesson that I learned after the fact.

It takes a lot of continuous work. It never ends. Either you're willing to do what it takes to remain connected or you're not. Some grandparents swallow their pride, and set their egos aside and get to work. Do they grovel? Yep. Do they eat crow? Heaps of it. Do they pound sand, till their hands ache? Does it work? Most of the time. Does it take a long time to regain access? Sometimes. And it absolutely requires patience and diligence.

There are grandparents who refuse, however. How dare they speak to me that way? I will not allow them to treat me this way. Why can't I take my grandchild to my house? Why do visits always have to be monitored?

The best advice I can share is do your best to put yourself in the other person's shoes, in this case the parent or custodial caregiver, and well probably anyone you're having difficulty getting along with. If you can do this, do so without malice. I'm not saying you have to agree with their behavior, what I'm saying is that is who they are. Believe them.

It does take work to truly understand what the other person is experiencing. People act the way they do because they believe they are doing the right thing. And people behave in the only way they know how. They behave the only way that they are capable of behaving. It's not always about us when people do the things they do.

"Side by side or miles apart, grandchildren are always close to the heart."

—Unknown

CHAPTER 14

Parental Authority And Case Precedence

THE CASE THAT I cited in Chapter 7 was also the precedence setting case that occurred just a few months prior to the one that I had been involved with, also in Casper Wyoming, and most probably had a significant influence on the outcome.

Sadly the grandparents lost the case.

In the April 2022 Wyoming publication, *Cowboy News Daily,* Jim Angell summarized the Wyoming Supreme Court ruling outcome in the case of Ailport v. Ailport, which bears repeating because of the direction the courts are taking:

"The rights of parents to raise their children as they see fit must be taken into consideration when grandparents ask courts to issue visitation orders for their grandchildren, according to the Wyoming Supreme Court.

The court on Thursday upheld a state district court's ruling against Jill and Shane Ailport, the grandparents of five children who asked a court to establish visitation rules for the grandchildren.

Supreme Court justices, in a unanimous decision authored by Justice Keith Kautz, said if the Ailports' request had been granted, it would have infringed on the rights of the children's parents.

Parents have a fundamental due process right to guide the upbringing of their children, including determining the level of contact with their grandparents, the ruling said, "... (State law) must be interpreted to protect parents' fundamental right by requiring grandparents to prove parents are unfit to make visitation decisions for their children or the parents' visitation decisions are or will be harmful to the children."

According to the ruling, the Ailports have two sons who have had five children of their own. In August 2019, "a rift developed between grandparents and parents." The opinion did not specify what caused the dispute.

A few months later the Ailports filed a petition to establish visitation rights with their grandchildren, relying on a state law that allows grandparents to seek such an order if they can prove visitation would be in the best interests of the children and if the rights of the parents would not be impaired by the order.

The parents of the children agreed visitation with the Ailports was in the children's best interests, but wanted to keep authority over when, where and under what conditions the visitations would occur.

The state district court ruled that the Ailports failed to prove they were entitled to a visitation order over the objections of the parents.

The Supreme Court upheld the decision of the state district court in Converse County, saying the grandparents were not able to prove why the court should interfere with the rights of parents in dictating visitation to a grandparent.

The Ailports were not able to provide evidence that the children would be harmed by the decision of their parents to retain authority over visits, the ruling said.

It added that evidence showed the parents had given the Ailports opportunities to visit their grandchildren on the parents' terms, usually at the parents' homes.

"Grandparents in this case did not meet their burden of establishing parents were unfit or made visitation decisions harmful to children," the ruling said."

A couple of things stand out in this case. First, it was only a few months after the "rift" that the grandparents ran to file a petition. It doesn't seem like there was a lot of time and energy put into solving the problem.

The second red flag is that the parents didn't flat out deny all access, but offered access on their terms. Again, they are the parents and the grandparents should not dictate the terms of visitation.

Both issues are examples of not spending time doing the behavioral work that is necessary to resolve the issue. Productive communication is a skill and requires education and practice. Anticipating consequences is a good tool to have as well. Most important is respect for parental authority. Clearly the grandparents did not take the least adversarial route. They jumped into a fight, not once but twice. They didn't accept the first outcome and escalated to a higher authority.

Closely related is the Troxel V. Granville case that became the ultimate grandparent-precedence-setting case and not in a good way, landing in the US Supreme Court in 2000. In Troxel v. Granville, the Supreme Court of the United States cited a constitutional right of parents to raise their children as they see fit. In other words they had parental authority to direct the upbringing of their children without interference. Citing infringement upon a parents' fundamental rights to rear their children, it struck down a Washington State law that allowed any third party to petition the state court to request child visitation rights over parental objections.

The ruling set a restrictive precedent for future grandparent visitation cases affecting all states. In Troxel, the grandparents wanted more than the parents were offering which ended up sadly for not only them and the children but for all grandparents who subsequently tried to go the legal route to obtain court ordered visitation.

ALSO CITED IS ROTH V. WESTON

In Roth v. Weston, a widowed father denied the maternal grandmother and aunt's request for visitation. The relatives challenged this decision, claiming that visitation was in the children's best interest; they did not contend that the father was an unfit parent. The father argued that visitation was not in his children's best interest and provided the trial court with evidence to support his position. The trial court ruled in the relatives' favor. Then it was appealed.

The Connecticut Supreme Court then reversed (Roth v. Weston, 259 Conn. 202 (2002)). It ruled that CGS § 46b-59, the state's third-party visitation statute, would be unconstitutional unless it required parties, including grandparents and other relatives, to make specific and good faith allegations to show that (1) they had a parent-like relationship with the child and (2) denying visitation would cause the child real and significant harm. The degree of harm had to be more than a determination that visitation would be in the child's best interest. It must be analogous to a claim that the child is neglected, uncared-for, or dependent within the meaning of Connecticut's child abuse statutes. Without this showing, courts lacked jurisdiction to resolve the dispute.

Once these high jurisdictional hurdles were overcome, the Supreme Court held that the petitioner had to prove his or her claims by clear and convincing evidence, a particularly stringent burden of proof. The Court indicated that these requirements affix a judicial gloss to the statute and serve as safeguards against unwarranted intrusions into a parent's authority (Roth v. Weston at 234-235).

The Roth standard is applicable to all third-party visitation cases brought in Connecticut.

In a motion filed by opposing council in the Wyoming case, the attorneys emphasized that a substantial and quasi-parental relationship was not there, nor had it ever been and that there wasn't evidence to support the finding worthy of governmental protection. They cited, Roth, 789 A.2d at 445 (Conn.2002) (severing of a parental-type relationship is different than a "**simply beneficial relationship,**" which is not "[t]he level of harm that would result from denial of visitation in such a situation is not of the magnitude that constitutionally could justify overruling a fit parent's visitation decision.").

The motion went so far as to state that court ordered visitation would actually create harm to the child.

What needs to change is consideration for children. Because they are minors, they have no voice in who they may love. They have no rights to be heard. Until that changes, judges most likely will follow the statutes. No one ever asks the question, what about the child? What does the child want? How will the child feel about losing access to Grammy and Papa?

What is hard to fathom is that while a judge may authorize a temporary visitation schedule until the case is settled, it could be removed once the judge rules in favor of the parents. That's exactly what happened in the Wyoming case.

This does not make sense. The child has become accustomed to scheduled visits whether weekly, monthly in person, by FaceTime, Skype or Zoom and simply because the case has ended it's taken away? Kids don't like change. Kids need structure. Kids need stability. Kids need security. Yet all of that is pulled away. What happened to best interests? How can this sort of action ever be in a child's best interest?

Everyone becomes enraged when a child is tortured by a parent. We have government facilities to protect children, even though that has been proven not always to succeed. Overloaded caseworkers allow child abuse cases to fall through the cracks.

Why does this happen? One reason is a non-biological adult is brought into the household. It could be a boyfriend, or a stepparent. It doesn't matter what the title is, what matters is that when this occurs, often times the extended family is cut off. These new additions tend to move in and take over.

I have seen it first hand and I have seen it second and third hand. My mother brought a man into our household, who altered our lives forever. Once they married, our home literally became this man's castle. His greatest accomplishment was ruling the roost with an iron fist. There was no hesitation in reminding us that he was head of the household. The house became a scary place now run by an iron fist following authoritarian rules.

Among those rules was keeping extended family away, except his. He wanted no reminder of Mom's former life, including her own parents along with my dad's parents. By keeping family away, he could isolate us and therefore do what he wanted without being scrutinized, or answering to anyone.

My visits with my grandparents became less frequent. I had been a direct pipeline and eagerly answered questions from grandparents, aunts and uncles. It's pretty common for kids to be quizzed about their home life from extended family, especially when there has been a disruption. That could also have contributed to fewer visits. Whether or not kids talk, the threat of sharing information is there.

Isolation has been found to be a common denominator with abusers. The news stories about children being abused, tortured and killed have all been cases where extended family has been out of the picture.

Beside lending a balance to a child's life, grandparents offer safety. I always felt safe when I was with my grandparents. I trusted them. I loved them and knew that they loved me. That secure feeling whenever I was around them was always present. Even when they visited our house, I always felt better when they were around.

My personal situation is an example of a dysfunctional household with periods of violence instigated by the non-biological adult. I can only assume that had extended adult family members such as grandparents been more involved there may have been some accountability.

I have heard second hand from grandparents who have experienced visitation issues following death and divorce of one of the parents where the surviving spouse cuts them off. Sometimes they do so as a single parent, not wanting a reminder of the past or not liking the in-law and using the opportunity to get rid of them. Other times, and most common is bringing the non-biological adult into the home. The surviving spouse will remarry and that person doesn't want the deceased parent's parent hanging around. In my seventeen years of counseling alienated grandparents this is a common theme. And truly heartbreaking. The grandparents have not only lost their adult child but also their grandchild. There is a finality about losing someone to death but not when you lose someone who is still alive. They are out there, somewhere, but out of reach. It's a horrible feeling. It feels like a missing person. The child, especially younger ones, are left living in a confused state of mind because they don't understand death and then why Grandma disappeared. The loss leaves an empty hole.

With a grandparent nearby, the hole doesn't seem so empty. They are a constant reminder of the parent that has died, which is comforting to still have a piece of that parent by the close proximity of the grandparent.

There have been cases where the parents divorce and one of the parents remarries and campaigns to push the former spouse away. It's hard when, lets say Dad, has relocated for work and visits the child less frequently. Sometimes the grandparents are kept at arms length rather than welcoming their presence since dad is no longer there on a daily basis. The visits become too hard for the child when the parents sabotage the grandparents. It's so uncomfortable for children to be placed in the middle that they have been known to withdraw from grandparents as a result.

What's good for the child is securing that gap with loving adults to build their self-esteem and character. Instead parents rip apart every last fragment of what has been established over time as a foundation. It comes tumbling down and the child is left with remnants of relationships. It's like pulling the rug out from underneath them and leaving them to fall.

CHAPTER 15

Family Law Attorney Contributes

LONI KLEIN, ESQ. Center For Children & Family Law, Orange California, who has extensive experience in grandparent visitation rights cases, expressed her frustration about the current status of grandparent visitation cases.

"Unfortunately, I am soured on grandparent rights cases right now as Judges are not being supportive of ordering the visitation. Even the strong grandparent rights cases wherein the child has lived with the grandparents, and they have acted in a caretaking roll in some capacity, have not been successful. It is disappointing and discouraging. The cases I have had recently the grandparents do not have the funds to appeal."

She explained that to show the loss of grandparent visits as detrimental to a child is a very high standard equating to state intervention which becomes so extreme.

"Judges just don't like these cases, they don't want to see conflict and defer to parent rights," said Klein. "Besides having busy calendars, it's the primary relationship between parent and child and why a judge won't take court time to mesh out conflict between adult child and their parent."

Attorney Klein suggested another possible consequence, based on her experience, is when grandparents file a petition for visitation. The outcome from filing actually ended up helping instead of further alienating the parents. "Sometimes filing can bring everyone to the table," said Klein. "The parties can mediate it and sometimes it does work, but don't wait too long."

CHAPTER 16

Grandparent Alienation Syndrome

GRANDPARENTS OFTEN LEARN, through the child, about the negative comments that the parents or caregiver have thrust upon them. Those grandparents who have court ordered visitation are able to diffuse and balance the field. Even so it's never good for the child to be subjected to the conflicting dialogue. But when the negative comments become a way of life and without the balance of having grandparents present, it becomes brainwashing.

In *Grand Wishes* I talked about grandparent alienation or GAS. The behaviors are akin to Parental Alienation Syndrome or PAS in that there is a concerted effort to brainwash the child against the other parent or, in this case, grandparent.

When grandparents are alienated from grandchildren for long periods of time there is a greater likelihood of this occurring. There is a greater chance that it can't be undone as well. The last grandparent story is an example of the extensive harm that occurs when a child is completely alienated through isolation and brainwashing.

JUDY AND ROGER

ALTHOUGH THEY ARE no longer married to one another, they are still parents and also grandparents.

Judy, along with her former husband, Roger, joined in a petition to file for court ordered visitation in Washington state where the grandkids had been relocated by their father after their mother was killed by a drunk driver. The father, still angry over the divorce, completely cut off the grandparents. The father left California without notice to the grandparents let alone anyone else, including the two dogs that were abandoned in the yard.

Judy finally got in touch with the dad and he agreed to let her come to Washington state for her granddaughter's 7th birthday. Then a misstep that could have triggered the dad's anger and alienation was the phone call that occurred during that visit when Judy had put her daughter Nicole, the child's aunt, on the phone to wish her a Happy Birthday.

The last contact Judy had had with her granddaughter was when she called after returning home. When it was time to say good-bye, the child said, "When can you come again, Grammy?" When Judy said in July for her brother's birthday, nearly nine months later, the granddaughter's response was, "Oh that's so long from now." The conversation was cut short when the little girl spilled something on the carpet and said that she had to go and clean it up because Daddy's going to be mad.

Judy and Roger went so far as to file a petition for grandparent visitation in the state of Washington where the children lived. They lost. It has now been 16 years since Judy has seen her grandchildren and not for lack of trying.

Judy did receive a call from her granddaughter when she turned 18 and when she tried to call her back it was as if her granddaughter had changed her mind about contacting her. Every time she called after that, the young woman was too busy to speak with her.

Aunt Nicole, wanting to be involved with her niece had actually been making some progress communicating with the young woman. She wanted to give her niece a window into her maternal family that had been taken from her. She compiled and sent her scrapbooks and albums with family photos. They had been communicating through video, chat app and texting but during one of their text exchanges, the girl became confrontational.

Nicole began the letter requesting a visit on behalf of her dad, Roger, the girl's grandfather, who was going to be in town. Her niece's response began by informing her that she and her husband were moving to Europe. She then admonished the aunt for sharing her phone number with the grandfather. The response escalated when the girl said, that she had no desire to to ever speak to her grandfather or anyone else from her mother's side of the family. She declared that she had painful memories of being manipulated by people in California.

The accusations directed to her grandparents (Judy and Roger) prompted her aunt to set the record straight. All future communication came to an end after that.

"You were 6 years old when the most tragic thing that could ever happen, happened. Your family from California rallied around both you and your brother out of love, not manipulation. Why would you even say that? You did not feel that way at age 6. That was a seed that was planted by your dad that you have chosen to believe. Unbelievable!!! That is so incredibly hurtful to say and it is quite apparent that you have been grossly mislead. We were all always there for you both, because we all loved you both and your mom!! Despite what happened between her and your dad, you two mattered most and no one manipulated either of you. It's so insulting to say and so callous of you to accuse your grandparents who did everything for you. Beforehand, and in the aftermath, you two were not the only ones that were hurting, but the ones that we could center our love upon. It is so sad that you have been brainwashed to think otherwise. Did you ever ask your dad how you ended up in Washington? How he never told any of us? How he put the house up for sale and took off without telling any of us? That he had it scheduled with me to pick you and Matthew up from school and I showed up very pregnant running around the school desperately trying to find you only to hear that you had not been in school for 4 days?

"He finally responded to our countless emails/phone calls months later to let us know you were both safe. Do you think that is praise worthy? I could only hope you would see that as cowardice on his part."

Nicole explained giving her dad the phone number but not home address according to the agreement between aunt and niece.

"Your grandpa did everything for you and your brother and I am sorry that your memories have been so altered that you have no memory of anything of your mom's side of the family that says otherwise. So very sad. There's two sides to every story, and you only have one."

It wasn't hard to figure out that the information didn't come from the granddaughter's memory. Her statement had come from being told untruths all those years about the maternal family that she had lost.

"I'm disappointed that they are now adults and still feel such hatred for us," said Judy.

"Every house needs a grandmother in it."

—Louisa May Alcott

CHAPTER 17

Words Of Wisdom

DR. LILLIAN CARSON shares her words of wisdom about the importance of the grandparent grandchild relationship during a speaking engagement on behalf of Advocates For Grandparent-Grandchild Connection.

"The first gift that we give our grandchildren is unconditional love. We're outside the daily grind and we don't have to worry as much about discipline, doctor's appointments, signing them up for soccer. We have a special position and that allows us to really give unconditional love. This love that we give them provides them with self-esteem and self-confidence closely linked to feelings of being loved and lovable.

We know now why some children who seem to have impossible situations in their life make it in spite of all that. And the reason that they do is because they have had a loving adult in their lives who believed in them. And that makes the difference. And as grandparents that is something that we are. Self esteem isn't something we lock up in the safe deposit box and have forever, it's like a bucket with a hole in it and some holes are bigger than others and it needs to be constantly replenished in order to stay healthy. The children need continual reinforcement, continual support, continual love from us.

An example is a story about the famous English actor Sir Lawrence Olivier. When a fan came up to him after a performance and said, 'Oh Sir Olivier I don't have to tell you what a magnificent performance you gave, I don't have to tell you how much pleasure you given to the audience, I don't have to tell you how much you mean to so many people and he simply replied, "You do, You do."

The second gift that we offer is modeling a good life, and we don't really have to do anything directly, but our children and grandchildren are watching us. They're watching the way we live our lives and our values. And if we live our lives with enthusiasm and purpose then they feel the future holds good things. If they see us deteriorating, depressed, not active, or embracing life then that sends a very sad and ominous message for them. We need to stay healthy not just for ourselves, but as a model because they are watching us.

The third gift is providing family continuity. We connect to grandchildren, to their history. We let them know that they belong to a family with a history and with roots. It is so grounding for them to know they belong to something greater than themselves.

There was a story from Kareem Abdul Jabbar, who talked about the stories that his grandmother used tell him. She told him that they were descents of great kings in Africa and he said, 'I knew that was in me and that helped me to believe in myself.' And you can almost feel what it would do for a child to feel that some greatness is in them and that therefore they could do so much more.

We need to create rituals, family meals, holidays keep showing up, just like we do. If you don't know your roots, if you don't know where you come from, it's much more difficult to know where you're going.

The fourth wonderful gift that we offer is insurance, stability and security. Family is a place that when you go there they have to let you in. And family is a place. My daughter, Susan, once told me, 'Grandma and Grandpa's place is like part of my compass; there's north, south, east and west, and Grandma and Grandpa's.'

I had the privilege of being an honorary elder of a native American joining ceremony. Part of that ceremony the shaman took the bride and groom around to each portal in a sacred circle and told them what their job was to be at at each juncture in the circle. When they came to my husband and me he said, 'and now you have become an elder and your job is to nurture the young.' That is our job; what a wonderful purpose it gives us. Because we need to live with purpose, without that life becomes a little drab.

And so we help our children, [grandchildren] to feel a part of the family. It gives them roots. We give them roots so that they can take risks and know that there is a helping hand if they fall down. We give them wings by letting them try out new things. It's a great thing. And when children are denied family bonds all that is lost to them. What a great pity for all of them.

And that's why were here today because we want to help as many children as we can to be able to enjoy the fruits that grandparents can offer.

But grand-parenting is also a slippery slope because we're not in charge.

A grandmother told me a story about her little grandson who was staying overnight and when she said, 'well it's 8:30, your mother told me that it was your bedtime, you have to go to bed.' He stopped and looked at her for a moment and said, 'but aren't you her mother?'

And there's the slippery slope, because we're not in charge anymore. That is very tough. Grandparents cannot drop out and not be missed. Our children are worth fighting for. That's why we're here to never give up. To keep finding a way and keep in mind the goal to do more. I will do more. I will do more than belong, I will participate. I will do more than care, I will help. I will do more than be friendly, I will be your friend. I will do more than be fair, I will be kind. I will do more than forgive, I will love. I will do more than earn, I will enrich. I will do more than teach, I will serve. I will do more than live, I will grow.

AND I ASK YOU ALL TO DO MORE.

"Parent-child relationships are complex. Grandmother-grandchild relationships are simple. Grandmas are short on criticism and long on love."

— Janet Lanese

CHAPTER 18

Some Things to Think About

RICK HARRISON, A Marriage-Family-Child therapist, before he died, provided a relevant quote to me that is worth sharing because it can be also applied to the parent-grandparent relationship:

1. CAN I CHANGE THE SITUATION?
Not all difficult people are beyond change, even though they are stubborn and stuck in their behavior. But there's a cardinal rule here that can't be ignored. No one changes unless he wants to. Difficult people rarely want to. If you have a close rapport with the person, you might find a moment when you can sit down and have a candid discussion about the things

that frustrate you. But be prepared with an exit strategy, because if your difficult person winds up resenting you for poking your nose where it doesn't belong, trying to effect change can seriously backfire.

Your best chance of creating change occurs if the following things are present:

- You have a personal connection with the person.
- You have earned his/her respect.
- You've discreetly tested the waters and found he/she a bit open to change.
- You've received signals that he/she wants to change.
- You aren't afraid or intimidated.
- The two of you are fairly equal in power. If the difficult person is in a dominant position, such as being your boss, your status is too imbalanced.

A final caveat. Difficult people aren't going to change just to make you feel better. The worst chance of getting someone else to change occurs when you're so angry, frustrated, and fed up that you lose your composure and demand change.

2. DO I HAVE TO PUT UP WITH IT INSTEAD?

When you can't change a situation, only two options remain, either put up with it or walk away.

Most of us aren't very effective in getting someone else to change, so we adapt in various ways. We are experts at putting up with things. Adaptation isn't bad per se; social life depends upon getting along with one another. It's a reasonable assumption that if you have difficult people in your life right now—and who doesn't— you've learned to adapt. The real question is whether you are coping in a healthy or unhealthy way.

Look at the following lists and honestly ask yourself how well you are putting up with your difficult person.

UNHEALTHY:

- I keep quiet and let them have their way. It's not worth fighting over.
- I complain behind their backs.
- I shut down emotionally.
- I don't say what I really mean half the time, for fear of getting into trouble or losing control.
- I subtly signal my disapproval.
- I engage in endless arguments that no one wins.
- I have symptoms of stress (headache, knots in the stomach, insomnia, depression, and anxiety) but have decided to grin and bear it.
- I know I want to get out of this situation, but I keep convincing myself that I have to stick it out.
- I indulge in fantasies of revenge.

HEALTHY:

- I assess what works best for me and avoid what doesn't.
- I approach the difficult person as rationally as possible.
- I don't get into emotional drama with them.
- I make sure I am respected by them. I keep my dignity.
- I can see the insecurity that lies beneath the surface of their bad behavior.
- I don't dwell on their behavior. I don't complain behind their backs or lose sleep.
- I keep away from anyone who can't handle the situation, the perpetual complainers, gossips, and connivers.
- My interaction with the difficult person has no hidden agenda, like revenge. We are here for mutual benefit, not psychodrama.
- I know I can walk away whenever I have to, so I don't feel trapped.
- I can laugh behind this person's back. I'm not intimidated or afraid.
- I feel genuine respect and admiration for what's good in this person.

If your approach contains too many unhealthy ingredients, you shouldn't stick around. You're rationalizing a hopeless situation. Your relationship with your difficult person isn't productive for either of you.

3. SHOULD I JUST WALK AWAY?

Difficult people generally wind up alone, embattled, and bitter. They create too much stress, and one by one, everyone in their lives walks away. But it can take an agonizingly long time to make this decision. The problem is attachment. The abused wife who can't leave her violent husband, the worker who is afraid he can't find another job, the underling who serves as a doormat for his boss—in almost every instance their reason for staying is emotional. Life isn't meant to be clinically rational. Emotions are a rich part of our lives, and it's mature to take the bitter with the sweet—up to a point.

Too many people stick around when they shouldn't. The main exceptions are competitive types, who can't bear to be dominated or made to look bad. They instinctively run away from situations that hurt their self-image. The other main personality types—dependent and controlling—will put up with a bad situation for a long time, far beyond what's healthy. The point, in practical terms, is that you can't wait until you've resolved all your issues with a difficult spouse, boss, boyfriend, buddy, colleague, or employee. Vacillation doesn't make you a better or nicer person. You are treading water, hoping that the dreaded day will never come when you have to sever ties. The thought of separation causes you anxiety.

But as anxious as you feel, sometimes a rupture is the healthiest thing you can do. That's the case if you have honestly confronted questions 1 and 2. If you know the difficult person isn't going to change, and if you've examined the unhealthy and healthy choices involved in putting up with them, you have a good foundation for making the right choice: Do I stay or do I walk? I'm not promising that your decision will feel nice. It probably won't. But it will be the right decision, the kind you will be able to look back on with a sigh of relief and recognition that moving on was healthy and productive.

CHAPTER 19

Conclusion

THIS BOOK CAME about after my experience as an expert witness in a grandparent visitation case that went to trial.

When I read that "grandparents are simply beneficial" in the motion that included references from the *Roth* case it struck a chord. Simply beneficial? First of all there is nothing simple about it and second what is opposite of beneficial? Harm. So how can an opinion such as this not be seen as hypocritical? I'll take a beneficial relationship over a harmful one any day.

The particular grandparent visitation case that I was involved in also tugged at my heart. The fact that the young child no longer had a grandfather and grandmother in his life at six years old was troubling. Clearly there was a bond. I keep seeing the boy's happy little face when he had his weekly scheduled FaceTime chats with the grandparents. It was obvious that he enjoyed the attention.

The grandparents fully engaged the child to make it all about him. The interaction was loving, fun and filled with laughter.

Just before the trial, a new video surfaced that portrayed the child in a completely different demeanor. The parents taped the boy crying and throwing a tantrum about not wanting to talk to the grandparents. The timing was suspect since this behavior had never occurred before in the three years of FaceTime calls with the grandparents.

There were indications of some coaching by parents that the grandparents observed during the visits. The occasional glances over his shoulder when he was talking, his programed answers when asked about certain things. The grandparents noticed some hesitation type behavior was present when parents were nearby.

I do not understand how a judge can rule in favor of visitation during the litigation process and take it away in the final ruling upon closing the case?

Granted the only access was FaceTime contact, but isn't that better than nothing?

Rulings such as this are becoming more prevalent. Grandparent visitation rights cases seem to be leaning more and more in the direction of denied court ordered visitation.

As Attorney Klein, stated, judges want to see

families work out their problems outside of court. The facts and laws in support of that position is PARENTAL AUTHORITY.

Our organization recommends that grandparents take the least adversarial approach. Only after putting forth the work that it requires to repair and maintain relationships, should grandparents seek legal counsel. It truly should be a last resort.

When the focus is on changing ones own behavior for the better the chances are higher that the results will be positive. Communication is key. Keep in mind that we as grandparents will do whatever is necessary to hold onto our beloved grandchildren.

"It's such a grand thing to be a mother of a mother—that's why the world calls her Grandmother."

— Unknown

OTHER BOOKS BY

Susan Hoffman

NON-FICTION BOOKS WRITTEN ABOUT GRANDPARENT VISITATION:

Grand Wishes: Advocating To Preserve The Grandparent-Grandchild Bond

A Precious Bond: How To Preserve The Grandparent-Grandchild Relationship

Grand Distance: Nothing Could Stop Her From Seeing Her Grandson Grow Up

Do You Want To Be Right Or Do You Want To Be Happy

FICTION BOOK ABOUT DOMESTIC VIOLENCE:

It Won't Happen Again: Home Becomes a Dangerous Place When A Monster Moves In

NON-FICTION BOOK FOR ALL AGES:

Diamond Is A Girl's Best Friend: And Why Life Is More Fun Sharing It With a Dog

"There is no greater sound than the sound of your grandchildren laughing."

— Unknown

ABOUT THE AUTHOR

Author Photo by Lawrence Sherwin

SUSAN HOFFMAN IS the creator and director of ADVOCATES FOR GRANDPARENT-GRANDCHILD CONNECTION, a 501 (c)(3) charitable organization. The purpose of the organization is to advocate on behalf of a child's right to maintain loving relationships with grandparents by providing resources to families, specifically grandparents experiencing visitation issues with grandchildren.

Susan sponsored a bill in California on behalf of grandparent visitation rights that became law in 2007. She resides on Balboa Island, California where she works as a freelance writer and also a journalist primarily contributing to the Los Angeles Times.

Proceeds from the sale of this book will be donated to Advocates For Grandparent-Grandchild Connection (AFGGC).

Made in the USA
Monee, IL
15 June 2023

35709980R00080